THE PLACE
CALLED
Heaven

JAMES T. JEREMIAH

Library of Congress Cataloging-in-Publication Data

Jeremiah, James T.
The place called heaven / James T. Jeremiah
87p.; 22cm.
ISBN 0-87227-150-1
1. Heaven—Christianity. I. Title.
BT846.2.J47 1991
236′ .24—dc20   90-25361
                                                          CIP

©1991
Regular Baptist Press
Second printing—1994

Printed in U.S.A.

Turning Point for God
Third printing—2005

DEDICATION

To the memory
of loved ones and friends
who are now rejoicing in
the Place called Heaven
and
To my wife Ruby and
the members of our family
who are, by the grace of God,
traveling to that Place called Heaven.

Foreword

One of the great heroes of my life is my father, James T. Jeremiah. My father's life was an example for me to follow on so many levels. He loved and served God with his whole heart. He was a man of integrity in every area of his life. He settled for nothing less than excellence as he faithfully served the Lord, preaching the Word for more than sixty years.

My father went to be with the Lord on August 7, 2000. Since his homegoing, I've reflected on the many life-gifts his legacy has given to me.

One of the greatest gifts was the last book he ever wrote, *The Place Called Heaven*. This book was almost as if he were leaving me a father-to-son letter, telling me about the place in which he now resides.

The Place Called Heaven is the product of a godly Christian life. My father's greatest example was his faith, and his legacy was one of tireless service.

He became president of Cedarville Bible College in 1959 when it had only 103 students. Today, the school has a student body of more than 3,000. Through all of my years growing up, I was able to watch my father demonstrate his faith and trust in God.

His lifetime of study produced numerous books, but *The Place Called Heaven* is my favorite.

It is my joy to share *The Place Called Heaven* with you. It will settle any questions you have about your eternal life, and it will equip you to minister comfort and hope to your own friends and loved ones who may have questions or anxiety about the "afterlife."

In its pages, you're going to discover, or rediscover, heaven as a real, not imaginary, place. You will also discover that it is a place of reunion and riches.

This book makes my heart soar because one of the things that my father and I shared was the focus in which we both dedicated our lives and ministry: pointing people to heaven.

I know one day my father and I will meet again. And as we embrace, standing on the streets of gold, the tears we shed will be tears of joy—a reunion made all the sweeter, knowing that we will never have to say goodbye again.

What a joy to spend eternity, never separated from my earthly and heavenly fathers! That is just one of the blessings I will eternally cherish in the place called heaven.

—David Jeremiah

Contents

Chapter

1   Heaven, a Place of Revelation 9

2   Heaven, a Place of Reality 13

3   Heaven, a Place of Righteousness 17

4   Heaven, a Place of Rest. 21

5   Heaven, a Place of Recognition 25

6   Heaven, a Place of Reunion 29

7   Heaven, a Place of Rejoicing 33

8   Heaven, a Place of Rewards 37

9   Heaven, a Place of Release 41

10   Heaven, a Place of Responsibility 45

11   Heaven, a Place of the Redeemed 49

12   Heaven, a Place of Riches. 53

13   Heaven, a Place of Refreshment 57

14   Heaven, a Place of Radiance. 61

15   Heaven, a Place of Royalty 65

16   Heaven, a Place of Reverence. 69

17   Heaven, a Place of Renewal 73

18   Heaven, a Place of Restriction 77

19   Heaven, a Place of Reservation 81

20   Heaven, a Place of Residence. 85

Heaven, a Place of Revelation

"Only the Bible Tells Us"

A fierce storm was causing havoc on the Great Lakes. A tugboat towing a barge began to sink. The captain and his shipmates took to a small boat. All night they tossed on the waves, constantly in danger of losing their lives. In the morning they were rescued by a passing ship. The captain afterward testified that there was one thing that gave strength to their arms as they rowed and kept them from losing hope. It was the lights of home they saw shining through the darkness and the storm.

In this world the Christian often sails through stormy seas, and he may at times be tempted to give up. He has hope, however, because he keeps his eyes on the lights of Home, the Bible promises about Heaven.

The unbeliever responds to this testimony by asking, "Do we really know anything for sure about Heaven? Is it not the figment of someone's imagination? Is it not more likely that Heaven was created in the minds of the deluded by some clever religionist or philosopher?" The answer is, "Yes, we do know something *sure* about Heaven. No, Heaven is *not* the imagination of some troubled soul; and *no*, Heaven was *not* created by man's clever mind." Heaven is a revelation from God, found only in the Bible, made known for our learning and encouragement. It is God's light from Heaven, not only telling us the way Home but what that Home will be like when we get there. It is the only authoritative source of knowledge about Heaven ever given to man.

CHAPTER 1

Since "all Scripture is given by inspiration of God" (2 Tim. 3:16), He is the author of it, and what He has revealed about Heaven is true and is to be believed. The uniqueness of this Book—its unity, teachings and power—all testify that it can be trusted. William W. Orr confidently stated, "Multiplied millions have already rested their entire future in its noted promises; nor are they deceived. This very day, many of them are enjoying the reality of what the Bible has taught to be true."

We know about heavenly things by written revelation. "But as it is written, Eye hath not seen, nor ear heard, neither have entered into the heart of man, the things which God hath prepared for them that love him. But God hath *revealed them unto us* by his Spirit: for the Spirit searcheth all things, yea, the deep things of God" (1 Cor. 2:9, 10).

The pages of Scripture reveal many wonderful things to us about our future home. This great revelation from God tells us about the believer's immediate future just minutes after he leaves this world by death. The apostle Paul, under the direction of the Holy Spirit, wrote: ". . . We are always confident, knowing that, whilst we are at home in the body, we are absent from the Lord: . . . We are confident, I say, and willing rather to be absent from the body, and to be present with the Lord" (2 Cor. 5:6, 8).

"For to me to live is Christ, and to die is gain. . . . For I am in a strait betwixt two, having a desire to depart, and to be with Christ; which is far better" (Phil. 1:21, 23).

While Stephen was being martyred for the cause of Christ, he called upon God and said: "Lord Jesus, receive my spirit. And he kneeled down, and cried with a loud voice, Lord, lay not this sin to their charge. And when he had said this, he fell asleep" (Acts 7:59, 60).

In the midst of this great trial Stephen "looked up stedfastly into heaven, and saw . . . Jesus standing on the right hand of God" (v. 55). Since Jesus is in Heaven and at death the believer is present with the Lord, then at death the Christian enters Heaven. The Bible and only the Bible makes this revelation about Heaven.

How Precious Is the Book Divine

How precious is the book divine,
By inspiration given:
Bright as a lamp its doctrines shine,
To guide our souls to heaven.

Its light, descending from above,
Our gloomy world to cheer,
Displays a Saviour's boundless love,
And brings His glories near.

This lamp, through all the tedious night
Of life, shall guide our way,
Till we behold the clearer light
Of an eternal day.

—John Fawcett, 1782 (1740–1817) Converted under George
  Whitefield's preaching, ordained a Baptist minister in 1764

Heaven, a Place of Reality

"More Than a Dream"

Heaven is a real place, much more than the "beautiful isle of somewhere" described by the poet. Before Jesus went to the cross, He promised, "I go to prepare a *place* for you" (John 14:2). The dictionary defines "a place" as a "definite location, or area occupied by or set aside for someone or something, with or without definite boundaries." The Bible uses several terms that fit into the meaning of this definition, indicating clearly that Heaven is a place of genuine reality.

1. Heaven is an everlasting *kingdom* for spaciousness. "For so an entrance shall be ministered unto you abundantly into the everlasting kingdom of our Lord and Saviour Jesus Christ" (2 Pet. 1:11). "Hearken, my beloved brethren, Hath not God chosen the poor of this world rich in faith, and heirs of the kingdom which he hath promised to them that love him?" (James 2:5).

2. Heaven is a better *country* for stability. "For they that say such things declare plainly that they seek a country. . . . But now they desire a better *country,* that is, an heavenly: wherefore God is not ashamed to be called their God: for he hath prepared for them a city" (Heb. 11:14, 16).

3. Heaven is a continuing *city* for security. "For he looked for a city which hath foundations, whose builder and maker is God" (Heb. 11:10). "But ye are come unto mount Sion, and unto the city of the living God, the heavenly Jerusalem, and to an innumerable

company of angels" (Heb. 12:22). "For here have we no continuing city, but we seek one to come" (Heb. 13:14).

4. Heaven is a divine *paradise* for serenity. "And Jesus said unto him, Verily I say unto thee, Today shalt thou be with me in paradise" (Luke 23:43). ". . . To him that overcometh will I give to eat of the tree of life, which is in the midst of the paradise of God" (Rev. 2:7).

5. Heaven is the Father's *house* for satisfaction. "In my Father's house are many mansions: if it were not so, I would have told you. I go to prepare a place for you" (John 14:2).

It is impossible to conceive of a kingdom, a city, a paradise, a country or a house without thinking of a real place. Heaven is a real place, a place of reality. It is much more than a dream of the "beautiful isle of somewhere."

Dr. Sanford F. Bennett, having served in the Civil War, returned to his home in Elkhorn, Wisconsin, to practice medicine. One day Joseph Webster, a close friend, visited him, but instead of chatting with Bennett he went over by the stove and sat alone. It was obvious that Webster had problems and was worried. After a time Webster looked up and said, "It will be all right by and by." Those words struck Bennett's mind forcefully, and he began to write: "There's a land that is fairer than day / And by faith we can see it afar / For the Father waits over the way / To prepare us a dwelling place there." Webster saw the doctor writing, so he got up and looked over his shoulder. Before long his despair left him, and he entered right into the writing of a song. Being a musician, Webster almost unconsciously began humming a tune we know today as the familiar song, "Sweet By and By." To the author and to us Heaven is "the land that is fairer than day." Have you made plans to spend eternity in that fair land?

Sing the Wondrous Love of Jesus

Sing the wondrous love of Jesus,
Sing His mercy and His grace;
In the mansions bright and blessed
He'll prepare for us a place.

Let us then be true and faithful,
Trusting, serving ev'ry day;
Just one glimpse of Him in glory
Will the toils of life repay.

Onward to the prize before
Soon His beauty we'll behold;
Soon the pearly gates will open—
We shall tread the streets of gold.

—Eliza E. Hewitt, 1898 (1851–1920)

Heaven, a Place of Righteousness

"A Sinless Society"

During World War II, a certain city in France was bombed and almost entirely deserted. A few houses were left standing, and among them was a luxurious dwelling. A few swine somehow had escaped death and rooted their way through a gap in the wall into this magnificently furnished home. Over the rich velvet carpet they tracked their muddy feet, overturned the upholstered furniture, tore the expensive draperies and chewed whatever gave any promise of satisfying their hunger. The beauty, the elegance, the cultural characteristics of the place meant nothing to the beast nature. They were not partakers of the intellectual or spiritual qualities of the owner. Pigs do not have natures compatible with a palace.

A New Nature Required. To the unregenerate millions of earth, the glories of Heaven would be like this beautiful home to the swine. They are not partakers of the divine nature and therefore would have no capacity for enjoying the atmosphere of Heaven. By nature they are prepared and by choice are headed for Hell. "But the fearful, and unbelieving, and the abominable, and murderers, and whoremongers, and sorcerers, and idolaters, and all liars, shall have their part in the lake which burneth with fire and brimstone: which is the second death" (Rev. 21:8). "For without are dogs, and sorcerers, and whoremongers, and murderers, and idolaters, and whosoever loveth and maketh a lie" (Rev. 22:15).

17

CHAPTER 3

The Word of God clearly teaches us that nothing tainted with sin shall ever enter into Heaven. "And there shall in no wise enter into it any thing that defileth, neither whatsoever worketh abomination, or maketh a lie: but they which are written in the Lamb's book of life" (Rev. 21:27).

A New Standing Provided. To live in the Holy City, we must have a holy standing before a holy God. The God of Heaven requires absolute perfection before we can enter Heaven. We have that perfection only in and through Jesus Christ. "Therefore being justified by faith, we have peace with God through our Lord Jesus Christ" (Rom. 5:1).

"Even the righteousness of God which is by faith of Jesus Christ unto all and upon all them that believe: for there is no difference" (Rom. 3:22).

"To the praise of the glory of his grace, wherein he hath made us accepted in the beloved. In whom we have redemption through his blood, the forgiveness of sins, according to the riches of his grace" (Eph. 1:6, 7).

A New Environment Guaranteed. A parishioner once asked an aged Puritan preacher, "Who will get to Heaven?"

The minister replied, "Every one will get to Heaven who can live there." Righteousness characterizes Heaven. It is called the Holy City. "And I John saw *the holy city,* new Jerusalem, coming down from God out of heaven, prepared as a bride adorned for her husband. . . . And he carried me away in the spirit to a great and high mountain, and shewed me that great city, *the holy Jerusalem,* descending out of heaven from God" (Rev. 21:2, 10). "And if any man shall take away from the words of the book of this prophecy, God shall take away his part out of the book of life, and out of *the holy city,* and from the things which are written in this book" (Rev. 22:19).

Heaven is a place of absolute righteousness, but God, through Christ, has made it possible for us to spend eternity there through the work Christ did for us. Have you accepted His righteousness? If you have, then you are made ready for that Holy City He has promised. At last the children of God will live in a perfect, sinless society!

When My Savior I Shall See

When my Savior I shall see,
In His glorious likeness be,
Clad in robes by love supplied,
Then shall I be satisfied.

When I'm wholly freed from sin,
Spotless, clean and pure within,
Meet to stand by Jesus' side,
Then shall I be satisfied.

Oh, till then be this my care,
More His image blest to bear;
More to conquer self and pride,
So shall I be satisfied.

—Peter Philip Bilhorn, 1887 (1865–1936)

Heaven, a Place of Rest

"Vacation at Last"

On earth we take vacations to find rest for our weary bodies and relief from our frustrations. For the child of God, Heaven will be an eternal vacation, not from service but from the troubles that plague our mortal bodies.

Someone has said that "death is paying a debt of nature." It is like exchanging money at the bank. At death, the Christian brings a crumpled note to the bank and obtains solid gold in exchange. When God calls one of His saints Home by means of death, the believer brings his cumbersome body, which he could not retain long anyway, and lays it down. He then receives in Heaven the eternal treasures of liberty, victory, knowledge, rapture and rest.

Promised. "And I heard a voice from heaven saying unto me, Write, Blessed are the dead which die in the Lord from henceforth: Yea, saith the Spirit, that they may rest from their labours; and their works do follow them" (Rev. 14:13).

"Just think of stepping on shore, and finding it heaven; of taking hold of a hand and finding it God's hand; of breathing new air and finding it heavenly air; of feeling invigorated and finding it immortality; of passing from storm and tempest to an unbroken calm; of waking up and finding it *Home!*" (Author unknown) Home—a place where we shall rest from all that has troubled, burdened or wearied us.

Experienced. While returning home late one night, a Scottish preacher observed a light in a lonely farmhouse on the moor.

Responding to a call for help, he found the farmer's wife dying. He pointed her to Christ, and just as the morning dawned, she went to be with the Christ Whom she had so recently trusted as her Savior. In speaking of this experience, the pastor said, "I found one in the kingdom of darkness; late at night, she entered the kingdom of grace; and just as the morning light dawned, she passed into the kingdom of glory."

"And God shall wipe away all tears from their eyes; and there shall be no more death, neither sorrow, nor crying, neither shall there be any more pain: for the former things are passed away" (Rev. 21:4).

Anticipated. Entering Heaven, the kingdom of glory, will mean rest for all of God's redeemed people. Some of them now eagerly await rest from suffering. When we enter Heaven, we will have no more pain or suffering. We shall rest from all of that and the many other burdens we carry on this earth.

Polycarp, a companion of the apostle John, suffered martyrdom on February 23, A.D. 155, at Smyrna. He knew something of the rest that awaited him when he entered Heaven. When he was arrested, he was asked, "What harm is there to say 'Caesar is Lord'?" He answered, "Eighty and six years have I served Him, and He has done me no wrong. How can I blaspheme my King who saved me?" He knew he would soon rest from his labors and could speak with assurance. "There the wicked cease from troubling; and there the weary be at rest" (Job 3:17).

As the psalmist has said, "Surely goodness and mercy shall follow me all the days of my life: and I will dwell in the house of the Lord for ever" (Ps. 23:6).

In Heaven the child of God shall rest from his problems and his pain. Now they remain a part of life, but we can have victory even here through the same Savior Who makes us fit for Heaven, where these troubles shall exist no more. Are you trusting Him now? On earth most of us look forward from one vacation to the next because our weary bodies always need rest but never find it completely. Heaven is the place where we shall have a rest that never ends.

Rest for the Toiling Hand

Rest for the toiling hand,
Rest for the anxious brow,
Rest for the weary, way-worn feet.
Rest from all labor now.

Rest for the fevered brain,
Rest for the throbbing eye;
Through these parched lips of thine no more
Shall pass the moan or sigh.

Soon shall the trump of God
Give out the welcome sound
That shakes the silent chamber-walls,
And breaks the turf-sealed ground.

'Twas sown in weakness here,
'Twill then be raised in power;
That which was sown an earthly seed,
Shall rise a heavenly flower.

—Horatius Bonar, 1857 (1808–1889)

Heaven, a Place of Recognition

"We Shall Know Each Other"

A Christian was once asked, "Do you think we shall know each other in Heaven?" The reply was, "Do you think we are to be greater fools in Heaven than we are on earth?" Naturally a great many people want to know where their departed loved ones are and whether they shall know each other in eternity. Several references in the Bible indicate we shall know each other in Heaven.

First, the Bible gives a specific promise that we shall know more in Heaven than we do on earth. "For now we see through a glass, darkly; but then face to face: now I know in part; but then shall I know even as also I am known" (1 Cor. 13:12).

Second, David expected to see and recognize his son who had died. "But now he is dead, wherefore should I fast? can I bring him back again? I shall go to him, but he shall not return to me" (2 Sam. 12:23).

Third, the rich man in Hell saw and recognized the beggar who had died. "And it came to pass, that the beggar died, and was carried by the angels into Abraham's bosom: the rich man also died, and was buried; and in hell he lift up his eyes, being in torments, and seeth Abraham afar off, and Lazarus in his bosom" (Luke 16:22, 23).

Fourth, Jesus promised that He would see the believing thief in Heaven. "And he said unto Jesus, Lord, remember me when thou comest into thy kingdom. And Jesus said unto him,

Verily I say unto thee, Today shalt thou be with me in paradise" (Luke 23:42, 43).

Fifth, Old Testament saints who long ago died shall be rec ognized in the kingdom of Heaven. "And I say unto you, That many shall come from the east and west, and shall sit down with Abraham, and Isaac, and Jacob, in the kingdom of heaven" (Matt. 8:11).

Sixth, we are assured the body placed in the grave will be recognized in the Resurrection. "So also is the resurrection of the dead. It is sown in corruption; *it* is raised in corruption: *it* is sown in dishonour; *it* is raised in glory; *it* is sown in weakness; *it* is raised in power: *it* is sown a natural body; *it* is raised a spiritual body" (1 Cor. 15:42–44a).

Seventh, the disciples had never seen Moses and Elijah, but they recognized them when they appeared in the transfiguration of Christ. "And, behold, there appeared unto them Moses and Elias talking with him. Then answered Peter, and said unto Jesus, Lord, it is good for us to be here: if thou wilt, let us make here three tabernacles; one for thee, and one for Moses, and one for Elias" (Matt. 17:3, 4).

William W. Orr suggests that in Heaven "we will seek an early introduction to some of the early church worthies—Polycarp, Athanasius, Justin Martyr, Augustine—and the leaders of evangelism in the early days—the Wesleys, Moody, Sunday— and the list of the missionary nobility is endless—Hudson Taylor, Judson, Livingstone—where can one stop? But we will meet them, every one." Some will tell of their cruel deaths. "And others had trials of cruel mockings and scourgings, yea, moreover of bonds and imprisonment" (Heb. 11:36).

The tragedy is that so many who wonder if they will recognize their loved ones in Heaven will not be there to experience personally that great joy. When the family circle is broken down here, it will not be mended up there unless or until those lost ones trust Christ to save them.

When the Mists Have Rolled Away

When the mists have rolled in splendor
From the beauty of the hills,
And the sunlight falls in gladness
On the river and the rills,
We recall our Father's promise
In the rainbow of the spray:
We shall know each other better
When the mists have rolled away.

We shall come with joy and gladness,
We shall gather round the throne;
Face to face with those that love us,
We shall know as we are known:
And the song of our redemption
Shall resound thro' endless day,
When the shadows have departed,
And the mists have rolled away.

—Ira D. Sankey (1840–1908)

Heaven, a Place of Reunion

"We Shall Meet Again"

Heaven is a place of reunion. This future meeting of God's children is so unlike our family reunion on earth. To begin with, all who will go to the reunion in Heaven have become God's people by being born into His family. No unsaved relatives will be there. Almost every year when the families of earth gather for their reunions, there are empty chairs. One or more of the family has entered eternity. No family reunion on earth ends without some sad farewells, but in Heaven no one will ever say good-bye. However, when God's people meet on earth, it is never for the last time, for they shall meet in Heaven if not again on earth.

Matthew Henry, the Bible commentator, was engaged to the heiress of a considerable fortune. Her father objected to his only daughter's marrying this Presbyterian preacher. "You see," he told her, "he may be a perfect gentleman, a brilliant scholar, and an excellent preacher; but he is a stranger, and we do not even know where he comes from!"

"True," replied the girl, "but we know where he is going, and I should like to go with him." When we know Christ as our Savior, we will spend eternity in Heaven with our loved ones who also know Him.

Christ has *prayed* to the Father that we may be with Him throughout eternity. "Father, I will that they also, whom thou hast given me, be with me where I am; that they may behold my glory, which thou hast given me: for thou lovedst me before the foundation of the world" (John 17:24). Who would dare say His prayer would go unanswered?

The Savior has *promised* that He will come to take us to live with Him. "And if I go and prepare a place for you, I will come again, and receive you unto myself; that where I am, there ye may be also" (John 14:3). Until that day dawns and we shall be transformed and bodily translated into Heaven, we know that the believers who depart this life in death will be with Him. "We are confident, I say, and willing rather to be absent from the body, and to be present with the Lord" (2 Cor. 5:8).

Our Lord has planned for our perfect reunion to take place when He returns. Then we will be with Him in our new bodies and will enjoy the reunion with all of our redeemed loved ones. "Then we which are alive and remain shall be caught up together with them in the clouds to meet the Lord in the air: and so shall we ever be with the Lord" (1 Thess. 4:17).

A man on his deathbed turned to his physician and mumbled, "What is Heaven like, Doctor?" How could the physician describe Heaven in such brief moments? As his mind searched for an answer for his friend, the doctor heard his dog scratching at the door. "Can you hear my dog scratching at your door?" inquired the physician. The sick man assured him that he could. "Well," the doctor said, "Heaven must be like that. My dog does not know what is in this room. He only knows he wants to be with me. So it is with Heaven! Our Master is there. That is all we need to know!"

To be in the presence of Christ is to be reunited with those we have loved and lost for a while.

What a Gathering

On that bright and golden morning when the Son of man
    shall come,
And the radiance of His glory we shall see,
When from every clime and nation He shall call His people
    home,
What a gath'ring of the ransomed that will be!

When our eyes behold the city with its many mansions bright
And its river, calm and restful, flowing free,
When the friends that death hath parted shall in bliss again
    unite,
What a gath'ring and a greeting there will be!

—Fanny J. Crosby (1820–1915)

Heaven, a Place of Rejoicing

"No Sadness There"

The Bible makes it clear to us that Heaven is a place of rejoicing. Since Christ will be there and always is the Source of joy, how can Heaven be anything else but a scene of eternal joy and happiness? When on earth, following His Resurrection, He said to His disciples, "Peace be unto you" (John 20:21).

Even at present our joy is found in Him. "And not only so, but we also joy in God through our Lord Jesus Christ, by whom we have now received the atonement" (Rom. 5:11).

D. L. Moody told the story about a little girl whose mother became seriously ill, and thus the little child was taken to the neighbors. The child had never been separated from her mother before, and she kept asking to be taken home. The mother kept growing worse, so the little girl could not return to her mother. Eventually the mother died. The grown-ups talked it over and thought it best to let the child remember her mother as she had known her, so the mother was buried without the little child seeing her. After the funeral the loved ones took her home, and the moment she got into the house she ran into the parlor and cried, "Mother, Mother." But Mother was not there. She went from one room to another, and then she began to weep and said, "Take me back." Home had lost all its sweetness and attraction to the girl.

What then would Heaven be like without Christ? Because Christ is there, Heaven knows no sadness.

Christ is the joy of Heaven. "Thou wilt shew me the path of life: in thy presence is fulness of joy; at thy right hand there are pleasures for evermore" (Ps. 16:11). While we wait to possess that joy in Heaven, we can experience some of it on earth. Jesus promised, "Ask and ye shall receive, that your joy may be full. . . . These things have I spoken unto you, that my joy might remain in you" (John 16:24; 15:11). He is the secret of our joy today as well as the assurance of our joy tomorrow. Then as now His joy will not depend upon the material things we possess: "For the kingdom of God is not meat and drink; but righteousness, and peace, and joy in the Holy Spirit" (Rom. 14:17). Heaven's joy is much more than happiness.

The great new song of Heaven will be sung to praise the Lord Jesus Christ. "And they sung a new song, saying, Thou art worthy to take the book, and to open the seals thereof: for thou was slain, and hast redeemed us to God by thy blood out of every kindred, and tongue, and people, and nation" (Rev. 5:9). The theme of the song sung in Heaven will be the worthiness of the Lamb of God.

When sinners repent and trust Him, there is joy in Heaven. "I say unto you, that likewise joy shall be in heaven over one sinner that repenteth, more than over ninety and nine just persons, which need no repentance" (Luke 15:7). "And they that be wise shall shine as the brightness of the firmament; and they that turn many to righteousness as the stars for ever and ever" (Dan. 12:3). Joy always comes when the lost is found, the sinner saved. The believer is made glad, the soul-winner rejoices and there is joy in Heaven in the presence of the angels.

He made Heaven the home of the believer. Those of us who are believers in Christ can bring rejoicing in the presence of the angels when we win those for whom He died. Yes, my Christian friend, you can have a vital part in bringing joy to Heaven.

Amazing Grace

Amazing grace—how sweet the sound—
That saved a wretch like me!
I once was lost but now am found,
Was blind but now I see.

And when this flesh and heart shall fail,
And mortal life shall cease;
I shall possess within the veil
A life of joy and peace.

When we've been there ten thousand years,
Bright shining as the sun,
We've no less days to sing God's praise
Than when we'd first begun.

—John Newton, 1779 (1725–1807)

Heaven, a Place of Rewards

"Honors Day Some Day"

Heaven is a place where God will reward the faithful: "Rejoice, and be exceeding glad: for great is your reward in heaven" (Matt. 5:12). A minister on the way to an appointment met another traveler. They talked together for some time. Finally the stranger said to the minister, "Sir, I think you must be on the wrong side of fifty."

"On the wrong side of fifty? No, sir, I am on the right side of fifty."

"Surely," the traveler said, "you must be more than fifty years old."

"Yes, sir, but on the right side; for every year I live, I am nearer my crown of glory."

The Bible specifies a *time* when God will reward His faithful servants. "And, behold, I come quickly; and my reward is with me, to give every man according as his work shall be" (Rev. 22:12).

". . . For we shall all stand before the judgment seat of Christ. For it is written, As I live, saith the Lord, every knee shall bow to me, and every tongue shall confess to God. So then every one of us shall give account of himself to God" (Rom. 14:10–12). No one has yet gone to his reward, *for the time of rewarding* has not yet come.

A clearly defined *basis* exists on which rewards will be given. Not all of God's people will be rewarded. Some will suffer loss of rewards (1 Cor. 3:15). God will reward His people in Heaven according to their faithfulness to Christ while they live and serve Him on earth. "If any man serve me, let him *follow me;* and where I am, there shall also my servant be: if any man *serve me,* him will my Father honour" (John 12:26).

"Blessed is the man that *endureth temptation:* for when he is tried, he shall receive the crown of life, which the Lord hath promised to them that love him" (James 1:12). "I have fought a good fight, I have finished my course, I have kept the faith: henceforth there is laid up for me a crown of righteousness, which the Lord, the righteous judge, shall give me at that day: and not to me only, but unto all them also that love his appearing" (2 Tim. 4:7, 8).

At the time we appear before the Judgment Seat of Christ, *we shall be examined* not to determine whether or not we are saved, but to reveal how we as saved ones have lived our lives for God. "If any man serve me, him will my Father honour."

Sometime after the rapture of the saints, God will offer several crowns to His faithful servants. One is the *incorruptible* crown for those who have, by His grace, mastered the old man (1 Cor. 9:25). Those who have been faithful soul-winners will receive a *crown of rejoicing* (1 Thess. 2:19). Those who have endured trials will receive a crown of life (James 1:12). As a reward for loving His appearing, a *crown of righteousness* will be given (2 Tim. 4:8). To the one who has served as a faithful shepherd and fed the flocks of God, the Great Shepherd will give a *crown of glory* (1 Pet. 5:4).

How will the rewarded believers *respond* to such an honor given in that day by the Lord Jesus Christ? In Heaven they will worship and honor Him by giving the crowns back to Him, as these crowns will not be for the eternal praise of the recipient, but for the honor and glory of the Giver.

What disappointment will be ours if we have no crown to give Him!

Must I Go, and Empty-Handed?

Must I go, and empty-handed,
Thus my dear Redeemer meet?
Not one day of service give Him,
Lay no trophy at His feet?

Not at death I shrink nor falter,
For my Savior saves me now;
But to meet Him empty-handed,
Thought of that now clouds my brow.

O the years in sinning wasted!
Could I but recall them now,
I would give them to my Savior—
To His will I'd gladly bow.

—Charles C. Luther, 1877 (1847–1924)

Heaven, a Place of Release

"A Better Day Coming"

On a cold, windy November day in England, a man spoke kindly to a poor Italian whom he had often passed without a word. Seeing him shiver, he said something about the dreadful English climate, which to a son of the sunny South must have seemed terribly cruel that day. But to his surprise, the man looked up with a smile and in his broken English said, "Yes, yes, pretty cold; but by and by, tink of dat." He was thinking of warm skies and flowers and songs in the sunny land to which he hoped soon to return, and he little imagined how all that day and for many a day, his words would ring in that Englishman's heart, "By and by, tink of dat."

An experience no one can avoid. In spite of the release of the "by and by," we are living in the "here and now," and trouble is an experience we cannot avoid. Heaven is the place where the children of God shall experience release from the bondage and the burdens of this world. In his first message to Job, Eliphaz described our lot when he said, "Man is born unto trouble, as the sparks fly upward" (Job 5:7). As surely as the sparks from a fire go upward, so surely the sons of Adam will have heartache. But for the child of God, a new day is coming.

An announcement no one can comprehend. God has made a promise to His children that goes beyond our understanding. As difficult, cruel and heartbreaking as our experience on earth may be, something glorious is coming for the people of God. Think of that. Heaven is not only wonderful because of Who and what will be there, but it is also wonderful because of who and what will not be there. In the future, before our eternal state begins, God will cast Satan out of Heaven. "There was war in heaven . . . And the great dragon was cast out, that old serpent, called the Devil, and Satan . . . was cast out into the earth" (Rev. 12:7, 9). What a promise for the residents of Heaven. Satan will no longer tempt, discourage or trouble them.

The Word of God promises us that in Heaven there will be no more "death, neither sorrow, nor crying, neither shall there be any more pain: for the former things are passed away" (Rev. 21:4). Sin and its awful consequences will be forever banished, for in Heaven "there shall be no more curse" (Rev. 22:3). "And there shall in no wise enter into it any thing that defileth, neither whatsoever worketh abomination, or maketh a lie: but they which are written in the Lamb's book of life" (Rev. 21:27). In Heaven the release from all of these troubles that now beset us will be so great that "the former shall not be remembered, nor come into mind" (Isa. 65:17). Who can comprehend all that is involved in this future place of glory?

Because we shall be released from all sorrow and pain, we have a message of *encouragement* that *cannot be duplicated* by anything man can promise or produce on this earth. With this knowledge of Heaven in our hearts, we can face trials of this life with the confidence that a better day is coming. This truth will also help us face eternity with new confidence and love.

J. G. Gilkey tells of a Greek by the name of Aristeides, who in about A.D. 125 wrote to one of his friends about Christianity. He tried to express the reasons this "new religion" was so successful. Here is a sentence from one of his letters: "If any righteous man among the Christians passes from this world, they rejoice and offer thanks to God, and they escort his body with songs and thanksgiving as if he were setting out from one place to another nearby." Christians can face eternity with serenity because they know they shall be released from the bondage of earth and liberated into the freedom of Heaven.

Meet Me There

On the happy, golden shore
Where the faithful part no more,
When the storms of life are o'er,
Meet me there;
Where the night dissolves away
Into pure and perfect day,
I am going home to stay—
Meet me there.

Here our fondest hopes are vain,
Dearest links are rent in twain,
But in heav'n no throb of pain—
Meet me there;
By the river sparkling bright
In the city of delight,
Where our faith is lost in sight,
Meet me there.

—Henrietta E. Blair

Heaven, a Place
of Responsibility

"Employees of Heaven"

A general, but false, concept of Heaven is one that promises an eternal place or state where the people who dwell there have no responsibility. William E. Biederwolf told of an epitaph that expresses this quite well:

> Here lies a poor woman who always was tired,
> For she lived in a place where help wasn't hired.
> Her last words on earth were, "Dear Friends, I am going
> Where washing ain't done, nor sweeping, nor sewing;
> And everything there is exact to my wishes,
> For where they don't eat, there's no washing dishes.
> I'll be where loud anthems forever are ringing;
> But having not voice, I'll get rid of the singing.
> Don't weep for me now, don't weep for me ever;
> For I'm going to do nothing forever and ever."

No, Heaven forever will be a place of service. About those who will be saved during the Tribulation and are in Heaven, John wrote: "Therefore are they before the throne of God, and serve him day and night in his temple" (Rev. 7:15). "His servants shall serve him" (Rev. 22:3).

If working for Christ brings joy to us now, why should we expect serving Him in Heaven will be any less enjoyable? If we serve "the living and true God" now and "wait for his Son from heaven," we shall rejoice at the privilege of serving Him throughout eternity. The opportunity of eternal service in Heaven should challenge us in working for Him on earth. An old Christian slave had the right attitude toward work:

> There's a King and Captain high who'll be coming by and by; and He'll find me hoeing cotton when He comes. You can hear His legions charging in the thunder of the sky; and He'll find me hoeing cotton when He comes. When He comes! When He comes! All the dead shall rise, in answer to His drums. Oh, the fires of His encampment star the firmament on high; and the heavens shall roll asunder, when He comes.

> There's a man they thrust aside, who was tortured till He died; and He'll find me hoeing cotton when He comes. He was spat upon and mocked at; He was scourged and crucified; and He'll find me hoeing cotton when He comes. When He comes! When He comes! He'll be loved by saints and angels when He comes. They'll be calling out "Hosanna" to the Man that men denied; and I'll kneel among the cotton—when He comes!

"Blessed is that servant, whom his lord when he cometh shall find so doing" (Matt. 24:46).

Since Christ died on the cross to save us so we can "serve the living God" (Heb. 9:14), why should we cease serving Him when this life on earth has ended? Since Christians have been "called . . . by love [to] serve one another" (Gal. 5:13) on earth, why should not their service be great in Heaven? When we were saved, we "turned to God from idols to serve the living and true God; and to wait for his Son from heaven" (1 Thess. 1:9, 10). So Jesus promised, "If any man serve me, let him follow me; and where I am, there shall also my servant be" (John 12:26). The Lord's servant will serve Him in Heaven in a more wonderful way than on earth.

People have speculated concerning what profession will have the best opportunities of service in Heaven. A newspaperman said at an American university, "They won't need doctors in Heaven because nobody will ever be sick there. They won't need preachers. Everybody there will have been saved. But people in the south end of Heaven will want to know what people in the north end are doing. They'll need newspapermen."

One thing is for sure—the only people who will live in Heaven are those who have heard and believed the good news of the gospel. Then they will serve their "Master in heaven" (Col. 4:1). Precisely what work we will do, what ministry of love, what errands for the Lord we will run or what studies we will pursue, not one of us can know as yet. But you can be sure Heaven is not a place of idleness.

From Every Clime and Kindred

From every clime and kindred
Arid nations from afar,
As serried ranks returning home
In triumph from a war,
I heard the saints uprising,
The myriad hosts among,
In praise of him who died and lives,
Their one glad triumph song.

And there no sun was needed,
Nor moon to shine by night,
God's glory did enlighten all,
The Lamb himself the light;
And there his servants serve him,
And, life's long battle o'er,
Enthroned with him, their Saviour, King,
They reign for evermore.

—Geoffrey Shaw, 1915 (1879–1943)

Heaven, a Place of the Redeemed

"A Body for Heaven"

When Thomas Titcombe started up the Niger River in
West Africa to do missionary work among the pagans, one of the
European traders on the river said to him sneeringly, "If these
pagans go to Heaven, I do not want to go there."

"They will be in both places," answered Mr. Titcombe. "I prefer
to go to Heaven with the redeemed ones."

Redemption denotes the means by which a person receives
salvation; that is, the payment of a ransom. "For even the Son of
man came not to be ministered unto, but to minister, and to give
his life a ransom for many" (Mark 10:45).

Someone has said that a preacher going through a mental
institution was stopped by a woman who asked, "Mr. Preacher,
what work of man will there be in Heaven?"

"None," said the minister.

"Oh, yes there will be," she said. "It will be the print of the
nails in the hands and feet of the Lord Jesus Christ. That is
the only work of man that will be in Heaven." Yes, how true this
is! The crucified Christ lives there, and by His atoning work He
has made it possible for others to live there with Him.

When Christ was crucified and resurrected, He provided
complete redemption for those who trust Him. Paul emphasized
this great truth in many of his epistles. "In whom we have redemption through his blood, the forgiveness of sins, according
to the riches of his grace" (Eph. 1:7). "Christ hath redeemed us

from the curse of the law, being made a curse for us: for it is written, Cursed is every one that hangeth on a tree" (Gal. 3:13).

This redemption of the soul also includes the body. In this life the believer's body is weak, often filled with disease and constantly in need of aid and repair. No Christian has a body now fit for Heaven, but the redemption purchased by Christ on the cross guarantees that every born-again person will have a body made ready for Heaven. "For we know that the whole creation groaneth and travaileth in pain together until now. And not only they, but ourselves also, which have the firstfruits of the Spirit, even we ourselves groan within ourselves, waiting for the adoption, to wit, the redemption of our body" (Rom. 8:22, 23; cf. Eph. 1:14).

The Bible teaches us that the body made fit for Heaven will be like the resurrection body of the Savior. "Beloved, now are we the sons of God, and it doth not yet appear what we shall be: but we know that, when he shall appear, we shall be like him; for we shall see him as he is" (1 John 3:2). "Who shall change our vile body, that it may be fashioned like unto his glorious body . . ." (Phil. 3:21).

When the Savior comes, He will raise the dead in Christ and change the living. "In a moment . . . the dead shall be raised incorruptible, and we shall be changed. For this corruptible must put on corruption, and this mortal must put on immortality" (1 Cor. 15:52, 53). The bodies of the saints will then be made incorruptible and fit for Heaven. When Jesus appeared to His disciples after the Resurrection He said to them, "Behold my hands and my feet. . . . A spirit hath not flesh and bones, as ye see me have" (Luke 24:39). He did not refer to a body of flesh and blood but to the body He has had since the Resurrection.

The assurance that the believer will have a new, glorified body without pain, sickness and infirmity, but made suitable for Heaven, comforts and encourages many of God's people (Rom. 8:16, 17, 21). When these bodies of ours become such burdens that we fall into deep despair, remember that they will be redeemed. This is as sure as the salvation of our souls can be and should be today.

Oh, What a Change

Soon will our Savior from Heaven appear;
Sweet is the hope and its power to cheer;
All will be changed by a glimpse of His face
This is the goal at the end of our race!

Loneliness changed to reunion complete,
Absence exchanged for a place at His feet,
Sleeping ones raised in a moment of time,
Living ones changed to His image sublime!

Sunrise will chase all the darkness away,
Night will be changed to the brightness of day,
Tempest will change to ineffable calm,
Weeping will change to a jubilant psalm!

Weakness will change to magnificent strength,
Failure will change to perfection at length,
Sorrow will change to unending delight,
Walking by faith changed to walking by sight!

—Ada R. Habershon (Copyright 1972 by Alfred B. Smith in
    Living Hymns)

Heaven, a Place of Riches

"No Thieves There"

Heaven is a place of unsurpassed wealth. When John had his vision of the New Jerusalem, he penned its description in the book of Revelation. He said, "The twelve gates were twelve pearls; . . . the street of the city was pure gold . . ." (Rev. 21:21). The light of the city is ". . . like unto a stone most precious, even like a jasper stone, clear as crystal" (Rev. 21:11). John saw that the twelve foundations of the city were made of twelve jewels, and he identified them. Think of Heaven being built upon a foundation made of stones such as jasper, sapphire, emerald, topaz, amethyst and other precious jewels. Indeed, Heaven is a place of great riches.

It is tragic indeed when many people turn their backs on Heaven, the place of eternal riches, because they are so enslaved with a passion to gain earthly riches that soon pass away. The Lord Jesus Christ commands us to do just the opposite. "Lay not up for yourselves treasures upon earth, where moth and rust doth corrupt, and where thieves break through and steal: But lay up for yourselves treasures in heaven, where neither moth nor rust doth corrupt, and where thieves do not break through nor steal" (Matt. 6:19, 20).

A man living in poverty was suddenly aroused from his dreams of better things by a loud knock at the door of his shack. The visitor at the door asked his name and if he had an uncle in England and other relatives by the same name in Australia.

When the answer was a rather hesitating yes, the man at the door replied, "Your uncle just died and has left you a fortune. Right now, most of the estate is in court, but you can have a down payment."

"How much?" the excited pauper asked.

"Only $5 million, but millions more will be yours in a few months."

In the light of what belonged to him now and the promise of more to come, can you imagine anyone so foolish as to insist on remaining a pauper when he could live like a millionaire? Yet some Christians live their spiritual lives as if they are paupers and will continue to be the poorest of people throughout eternity. The Word of God has much to say about the inheritance of the saints. "Giving thanks unto the Father, which hath made us meet to be partakers of the inheritance of the saints in light" (Col. 1:12). "And whatsoever ye do, do it heartily, as to the Lord, and not unto men; knowing that of the Lord ye shall receive the reward of the inheritance: for ye serve the Lord Christ" (Col. 3:23, 24).

The apostle Peter reminds us that the children of God have been "begotten . . . again unto a [living] hope . . . to an inheritance" (1 Pet. 1:3, 4). The Bible teaches that this inheritance is

1. *Beyond death.* It is "incorruptible" as to its endurance. It is beyond decay. There is no autumn in it. Its climate never changes. Its value never decreases.

2. *Beyond defilement.* It is "undefiled" as to its purity. On earth everything has flaws and imperfections. In Heaven nothing enters to defile—and that includes our inheritance.

3. *Beyond degeneration.* It is "unfading" as to its beauty. People change on earth. Look at your picture taken twenty-five years ago and be persuaded. Our inheritance in Heaven never fades.

4. *Beyond destruction.* It is "reserved" as to its security. Nothing is sure on earth. Thieves steal. Rust corrupts. Sin ruins. Our inheritance in Heaven is indestructible.

Why do we put so much effort on gaining riches of this earth when we cannot keep them and forfeit the riches of Heaven that

we cannot lose once we have gained them? "Lay not up for yourselves treasures upon earth . . . where thieves break through and
steal: but lay up . . . in heaven . . . where thieves do not break
through nor steal" (Matt. 6:19, 20). Heaven is the only place to
put riches if we want to keep them.

A Child of the King

My Father is rich in houses and lands,
He holdeth the wealth of the world in His hands!
Of rubies and diamonds, of silver and gold,
His coffers are full—He has riches untold.

My Father's own Son, the Savior of men,
Once wandered o'er earth as the poorest of them;
But now He is reigning forever on high,
And will give me a home in heav'n by and by.

I once was an outcast stranger on earth,
A sinner by choice and an alien by birth;
But I've been adopted, my name's written down—
An heir to a mansion, a robe and a crown.

A tent or a cottage, why should I care?
They're building a palace for me over there!
Tho exiled from home, yet, still I may sing:
All glory to God, I'm a child of the King!

—Hattie E. Buell, 1877 (1834–1910)

Heaven, a Place of Refreshment

"Fresh Air at Last"

In comparison to the wilderness of this earth, Heaven is a place of eternal refreshment. To be refreshed is to be revived as with rest, food or drink. Now at very best, ". . . we see through a glass, darkly. . . . Now I know in part; but then . . ." (1 Cor. 13:12) what a difference it will be!

A little boy who had never visited the country before was amazed at what he saw. He had never been beyond the narrow streets of the city with its walls of buildings on either side. When he got out into the country, he cried, "Oh! Oh! Oh!" His hostess asked the reason for the outburst. The boy replied. "Why, what a big sky you have out here!" With unobstructed view he, for the first time, had seen the "sky." When we have left behind all the material structures that now obscure and limit our vision and we enter Heaven, we shall exclaim, "Oh! What a great Savior He is."

Heaven will be sufficient. When the saints of God enter the Heaven He has prepared for them, they will be amazed and refreshed by the sight of that perfectly pure place. It will be all that anyone has expected and more. We can only imagine what a refreshing place Heaven is and for all eternity will be. The apostle John saw it and, by the inspiration of the Holy Spirit, has described this aspect of the heavenly city for us. He said, "He showed me a *river* of the water of life, clear as crystal, coming from the throne of God and of the Lamb, in the middle of its

57

street. And on either side of the river was the *tree* of life, bearing twelve kinds of *fruit,* yielding its fruit every month; and the leaves of the tree were for the healing of the nations. And there shall *no* longer be any curse" (Rev. 22:1–3, NASB).

Heaven will sustain its residents. How often citizens of large cities have been asked during dry summer months to use water sparingly. This reminds us that a city without water would soon be destroyed. But that city will have no water shortage because a river will proceed out of the throne of God in an abundant supply. Water in this passage has been interpreted to mean baptism, the Holy Spirit, the influence of the Church on the world; but it simply means what it says—"the water of life." It will be there in abundance, for it is "a pure river of the water of life." The psalmist may have had this "pure river" in mind when he wrote, "There is a river, the streams whereof shall make glad the city of God, the holy place of the tabernacles of the most high" (Ps. 46:4).

Heaven will be satisfying. The Garden of Eden had "the tree of life . . . and the tree of knowledge of good and evil" (Gen. 2:9). Man ate of the latter and died spiritually and physically. The tree of life in that heavenly city assures us of the eternal abundance of life for the people of God. "It is the beautiful symbol of life in its gladness, purity, and fullness." What a refreshing place Heaven will be! The river of life sustains the believer in Heaven, and the tree of life satisfies him.

Heaven will be a place most secure. Sin entered the Garden of Eden and brought a curse upon this paradise of God. In Heaven God's people will be forever secure from any attacks of sin. "There shall be no more curse." Any city on earth has abundant examples of the curse. Policemen, judges, jails, hospitals, undertakers and cemeteries—all witness the fact that the curse of sin is still with us. The heavenly city, the New Jerusalem, will have light and food and water, the essentials to sustain life forever. Why then sell your soul for the empty things of earth that satisfy, if at all, but for a brief time?

Beautiful Zion

Beautiful Zion, built above,
Beautiful city that I love:
Beautiful gates of pearly white!
Beautiful temple, God is light!

Beautiful trees forever there,
Beautiful fruits that always bear;
Beautiful river gliding by,
Beautiful fountain never dry!

Beautiful heaven where all is light,
Beautiful angels clothed in white;
Beautiful songs that never tire,
Beautiful harps thro' all the choir!

—J. H. Tenny

Heaven, a Place of Radiance

"Like the Firmament's Brightness"

Who on this earth can imagine what the light of Heaven is like? It is all light, no night or darkness. It is a place of glorious, radiating light. The dictionary defines radiance as brightness shooting in rays or beams; brilliant or sparkling luster; vivid brightness, as the radiance of the sun." Synonyms of radiance are brilliance, luster, splendor and resplendence. These words help us to comprehend the sight of Heaven.

In the book of the Revelation the apostle John reported that one of the seven angels "carried me away in the spirit to a great and high mountain, and shewed me that great city, the holy Jerusalem, descending out of heaven from God, having the glory of God: *and her light was like unto a stone most precious,* even like a jasper stone, clear as crystal" (Rev. 21:10, 11). The Bible further reveals that "the city had no need of the sun, neither of he moon, to shine in it: for the glory of God did lighten it, and the Lamb is the light thereof" (v. 23).

W. A. Criswell described this radiance of the heavenly city saying, "The garments of God reflect the glory, iridescence, the incomparable effusion of beauty, color, splendor and light that stream from His Person. . . . There is an inherent light and glory in the city because Jesus is there, and the Lamb is the light thereof. All light, hope and blessing stream from His blessed face" (*Expository Sermons on Revelation*, vol. 5, p. 131).

When Moses went into the presence of God and came down from Mount Sinai with the Ten Commandments, he knew "not that the skin of his face shone while he talked with him. . . . They were afraid to come nigh him. . . . And Moses put the vail upon his face again" (Exod. 34:29, 30, 35). The Transfiguration revealed the glory of the Lord Jesus Christ, "and his face did shine as the sun, and his raiment was white as the light" (Matt. 17:2). Here is a brief glance of the brilliance of Heaven come to earth. When Saul of Tarsus went on his way to Damascus with the plan to persecute the Christians, "suddenly there shined round about him a light from heaven" (Acts 9:3).

No shadows will be in Heaven because it will have perfect and complete light. "God is light and in him is no darkness at all" (1 John 1:5). The "valley of the shadow of death" therefore of necessity must be on earth. In fact, every day we live we are walking, driving or flying in that valley. In contrast, no shadows will be in Hell either, for the Bible describes that awful place as "the blackness of darkness for ever" (Jude 13).

While on each, Jesus said, "I am the light of the world: he that followeth me shall not walk in darkness, but shall have the light of life" (John 8:12). He came as the high priest from Heaven, and like John the Baptist, God's people are "to bear witness of the Light, that all men through him might believe" (John 1:7). Then they "shall shine as the brightness of the firmament; and they that turn many to righteousness as the stars for ever and ever" (Dan. 12:3).

God will not need man's efforts to make Heaven what it will be throughout eternity. He has given His people the opportunity to serve on earth in a way that will eventually make us a part of the glories of Heaven. In turning many to Christ for salvation, the believer is assured of shining like the brightness of the firmament. God's faithful witnesses will then blend into the radiance of Heaven.

No Need of the Sun

No need of the sun in that day
Which never is follow'd by night,
Where Jesus' beauties display
A pure and a permanent light:
The Lamb is their Light and their Sun,
And, lo! by reflection they shine;
With Jesus ineffably one,
And bright in effulgence divine.

The saints in His presence receive
Their great and eternal reward;
In Jesus, in heaven, they live—
They reign in the smile of their Lord.
The flame of angelic love
Is kindled at Jesus' face;
And all the enjoyment above,
Consists in the rapturous gaze.

—Charles Wesley (1707–1788)

Heaven, a Place of Royalty

"God's Throne Room"

The Bible says that God's throne is in Heaven: "The LORD hath prepared his throne in the heavens; and his kingdom ruleth over all" (Ps. 103:19). "The LORD is in his holy temple, the LORD's throne is in heaven" (Ps. 11:4). Isaiah reported God saying, "The heaven is my throne, and the earth is my footstool" (Isa. 66:1). He is "the King of heaven" (Dan. 4:37). Repeatedly Solomon prayed, "Hear thou in heaven thy dwelling place" (1 Kings 8:30, 39, 43, 45, 49).

The God whose throne is in Heaven is the King of Heaven and earth. "The earth is the LORD's, and the fulness thereof; the world, and they that dwell therein. . . . Who is this King of glory? The LORD of hosts, he is the King of glory. Selah" (Ps. 24:1, 10). "The heavens are thine, the earth also is thine: as for the world and the fulness thereof, thou hast founded them. . . . For the LORD is our defence; and the Holy One of Israel is our king" (Ps. 89:11, 18). "But the LORD is the true God, he is the living God, and an everlasting king: at his wrath the earth shall tremble, and the nations shall not be able to abide his indignation" (Jer. 10:10).

When the children of God leave this world, they shall spend eternity in the presence of royalty. Upon entering Heaven, the throne room of God, His people shall as never before know and appreciate His:

Presence—"Therefore are they before the throne of God, and serve him day and night in his temple: and he that sitteth on the throne shall dwell among them" (Rev. 7:15).

Power—"And he that sat upon the throne said, Behold, I make all things new. And he said unto me, Write: for these words are true and faithful" (Rev. 21:5). ". . . O LORD God of our fathers, art not thou God in heaven? and rulest not thou over all the kingdoms of the heathen? and in thine hand is there not power and might, so that none is able to withstand thee?" (2 Chron. 20:6).

Provision—"And he said unto me, It is done. I am Alpha and Omega, the beginning and the end. I will give unto him that is athirst of the fountain of the water of life freely" (Rev. 21:6). "Blessed are they that do his commandments, that they may have right to the tree of life, and may enter in through the gates into the city" (Rev. 22:14).

Possessions—"Therefore let no man glory in men. For all things are yours; . . . and ye are Christ's; and Christ is God's" (1 Cor. 3:21, 23). ". . . For all that is in the heaven and in the earth is thine; thine is the kingdom, O LORD, and thou art exalted as head above all. Both riches and honour come of thee, and thou reignest over all; and in thine hand is power and might; and in thine hand it is to make great, and to give strength unto all" (1 Chron. 29:11, 12).

Protection—"Because thou hast kept the word of my patience, I also will keep thee from the hour of temptation, which shall come upon all the world, to try them that dwell upon the earth" (Rev. 3:10).

In a small, relatively insignificant way the saints of God on earth come to know and appreciate what it means to have the blessings of our sovereign God. In Heaven, in the eternal presence of Royalty, the King of Kings, we shall be what we now are in Christ, sons and daughters of our great King. Jesus promised, "To him that overcometh will I grant to sit with me in my throne, even as I also overcame, and am set down with my Father in his throne" (Rev. 3:21).

When I Can Read My Title Clear

When I can read my title clear
To mansions in the skies,
I'll bid farewell to ev'ry fear,
And wipe my weeping eyes.

Should earth against my soul engage,
And fiery darts be hurled,
Then I can smile at Satan's rage,
And face a frowning world.

Let cares, like a wild deluge come,
And storms of sorrow fall!
May I but safely reach my home,
My God, my heav'n, my all.

There shall I bathe my weary soul
In seas of heav'nly rest,
And not a wave of trouble roll
Across my peaceful breast.

—Isaac Watts, 1707 (1674–1748)

CHAPTER 16

Heaven, a Place of Reverence

"Every Knee Shall Bow"

Heaven is a place where every resident will bow down and worship the Christ Who redeemed him. It is and will be a place of reverence, a place of profound awe, respect and worship. A young seminary student was once called to the deathbed of a faithful old soldier of the Cross. The young man sought to comfort the aged saint as he faced the last and inevitable hour. He read to him from chapter 14 of John, verse 2: "In my Father's house are many mansions: if it were not so, I would have told you. I go to prepare a place for you." The young man stopped reading and began speaking to the aged Christian about the glorious mansion in the sky. As he spoke, the old pilgrim placed his hand on the young man's arm and said, "No, no, my son, read on. Read the third verse," So the young man continued, "If I go and prepare a place for you, I will come again, and receive you unto myself; that where I am, there ye may be also." The aged saint said, "Son, what is it! That is it! It is not a mansion in the skies or streets of gold beyond pearly gates that these old eyes are longing to see. It is my Savior I want so much to see. It will be Heaven enough to love Him and to be with Him."

J. Dwight Pentecost said, "There is the danger that the redeemed one will become so occupied with the anticipation of his own experience of glory that the supreme glorification of the Godhead is lost. Our occupation in the eternal state will not be with our position or glory, but with God Himself" (*Things to Come* [Findlay, OH: Dunham Publishing Company, 1958], p. 582). As glorious as the radiance and riches of Heaven will be, the sight of the Redeemer will make the sight of all we shall view around us to be of less importance to the believer.

We shall see Him. "Beloved, now are we the sons of God, and it doth not yet appear what we shall be: but we know that, when he shall appear, we shall be like him; for *we shall see him as he is*" (1 John 3:2). "Behold, he cometh with clouds; and *every eye shall see him,* and they also which pierced him: and all kindreds of the earth shall wail because of him. Even so, Amen" (Rev. 1:7).

We anticipate that the first One we shall see in Heaven will be the Lord Jesus Christ. We shall see Him as He is described by John in Revelation 1:13-15: "And in the midst of the seven candlesticks one like unto the Son of man, clothed with a garment down to the foot, and girt about the paps with a golden girdle. His head and his hairs were white like wool, as white as snow; and his eyes were as a flame of fire; And his feet like unto fine brass, as if they burned in a furnace; and his voice as the sound of many waters." These verses paint the only authentic portrait of Christ as He is and as He will be. No artist on earth has or will ever match it!

We shall worship Him. "Worthy is the Lamb that was slain to receive power, and riches, and wisdom, and strength, and honour, and glory, and blessing. . . And the four and twenty elders fell down and *worshipped him* that liveth for ever and ever" (Rev. 5:12, 14). "And I John saw these things, and heard them. And when I had heard and seen, I fell down to worship before the feet of the angel which shewed me these things. Then saith he unto me, See thou do it not: for I am thy fellowservant, and of thy brethren the prophets, and of them which keep the sayings of this book: *worship God"* (Rev. 22:8, 9).

Anne Ross Cousin wrote in her song "The Sands of Time Are Sinking": "The Bride eyes not her garment / But her dear bridegroom's face / I will not gaze on glory / But on my King of Grace. Not at the crown He giveth / But on His pierced hand / The Lamb is all the glory / Of Immanuel's land."

In Heaven we shall spend eternity worshiping our Lord and Savior. Don't you suppose it would be a good thing to begin worshiping Him now? When you know Him as your Savior, you will bow before Him as your Lord and King.

The God of Abraham Praise

The God of Abraham praise,
Who reigns enthroned above,
Ancient of everlasting days,
And God of love.
Jehovah, great I AM,
By earth and heav'n confessed,
I bow and bless the sacred Name
Forever blest.

He by Himself hath sworn—
I on His oath depend;
I shall, on eagles' wings upborne,
To heav'n ascend;
I shall behold His face,
I shall His pow'r adore,
And sing the wonders of His grace
Forevermore.

The whole triumphant host
Give thanks to God on high;
"Hail, Father, Son and Holy Ghost!"
They ever cry.
Hail, Abraham's God and mine!
I join the heavenly lays;
All might and majesty are Thine,
And endless praise.

—Thomas Olivers, 1770 (1725–1799)

Heaven, a Place of Renewal

"All Things New"

Heaven will be characterized by many new things. To "renew" means "to make new or as if new again; restore or replenish." Jesus said, "Behold, I make all things new" (Rev. 21:5).

In prophetic reference to Israel, the prophet Isaiah quoted God's promise when he wrote, "Behold, I create new heavens and a new earth: and the former shall not be remembered, nor come into mind" (Isa. 65:17). Peter affirmed, "We, according to his promise, look for new heavens and a new earth, wherein dwelleth righteousness" (2 Pet. 3:13). John wrote as though the prophecy had been fulfilled: "And I saw a new heaven and a new earth: for the first heaven and the first earth were passed away" (Rev. 21:1).

The Bible teaches that there are three heavens. First is the atmospheric heaven that surrounds our earth. Then there is the planetary heaven where the sun, moon and stars move. The third heaven is the place where the redeemed go when they depart this world by death. Paul refers to being "caught up to the third heaven" (2 Cor. 12:2).

Nothing has or ever will defile the Heaven that is God's abode. The heavens polluted by Satan are to be renewed, for they are not "clean in his [God's] sight" (Job 15:15). Satan is now "the prince of the power of the air" (Eph. 2:2). He brought "spiritual wickedness" into the heavenlies (6:12). As God renovated the earth by water in Noah's day, so He will renovate the earth and the stellar heavens by fire in a yet future time. "The heavens and the earth, which are now . . . are kept in store, reserved unto fire" (2 Pet. 3:7).

After a vision of "a new heaven and a new earth," John saw the New Jerusalem. When Christ makes "all things new," "the tabernacle of God is with men, and he will dwell with them" (Rev. 21:3). The old, unhappy experience of this present life will be ended, for there shall be no more tears, death, crying or pain. Dr. Leon Tucker said the book of Romans is the book of "much mores," and the book of Revelation is the book of "no mores." When all things are made new, we will have complete satisfaction because we can drink of the fountain of the water of life (v. 6), and then we shall inherit all things (v. 7). Those who habitually walk in sin because they have not been made a new creation (2 Cor. 5:17) will not have a part in Heaven, but in "the lake which burneth with fire" (Rev. 21:8).

People who passed Lord Rothschild's mansion in Piccadilly, London, were surprised to notice that the end of one of the cornices of his beautiful home was unfinished. Many thought it strange that a rich man such as he could not afford to put the final touches on this otherwise elegant residence. The explanation, however, was simple. Lord Rothschild was an orthodox Jew, and every pious Jew's house, tradition says, must have some part unfinished to bear testimony to the fact that its occupants, like Abraham, are but pilgrims and strangers on earth. The incomplete cornice on the mansion says to all who understand its meaning: "This is not Lord Rothschild's final home; he is traveling to eternity."

When we enter that heavenly home and experience that unspeakable blessing when "all things are made new," we shall know the meaning of absolute completeness and fulfillment. Since our God is finishing our Heaven, preparing dwelling places for us, He will also finish us completely for our finished home.

A City Yet to Come

This is not my place of resting,
Mine's a city yet to come;
Onward to it I am hasting,
On to my eternal home.
In it all is light and glory;
O'er it shines a nightless day;
Every trace of sin's sad story,
All the curse, hath passed away.

There the Lamb, our Shepherd, leads us,
By the streams of life along,
On the freshest pastures feeds us,
Turns our sighing into song.

Soon we pass this desert dreary,
Soon we bid farewell to pain;
Never more are sad or weary,
Never, never sin again.

—Horatius Bonar, 1845 (1808–1889)

Heaven, a Place of Restriction

"Don't Expect It Here"

Many believe that if Heaven exists at all, every person who dies goes there. No one, according to this point of view, is ever lost. We are told that all of us are children of God and God is the Father of all. A loving God, they say, will not permit any of His creation to go to Hell, so consequently everyone at death must go to Heaven, if Heaven there be. Three words describe Heaven's restrictions: limitation, separation and rejection.

Limitation—Several passages of Scripture suggest that Heaven is a place of restriction. There are bounds over which some of Adam's race cannot pass. To begin with, Heaven is limited to only those who have been redeemed by Christ. "For Christ also hath once suffered for sins, the just for the unjust, that he might bring us to God, being put to death in the flesh, but quickened by the Spirit" (1 Pet. 3:18). Jesus said, "Rejoice, because your names are written in heaven" (Luke 10:20). That statement strongly suggests that some names are not written in Heaven. The Word of God also states that "whosoever was not found written in the book of life was cast into the lake of fire" (Rev. 20:15).

Separation—Several statements in Scripture emphasize that in eternity the righteous in Christ shall be separated from the ungodly. "So shall it be at the end of the world: the angels shall come forth, and sever the wicked from among the just" (Matt. 13:49). No one who would defile Heaven can ever enter there. Heaven is restricted to God's people, and Hell is reserved for the ungodly.

To make this point even stronger, the Bible gives several lists of sinners who will not be in Heaven. "Or do you not know that the unrighteous shall not inherit the kingdom of God? Do not be deceived; neither fornicators, nor idolaters, nor adulterers, nor effeminate, nor homosexuals, nor thieves, nor covetous, nor drunkards, nor revilers, nor swindlers, shall inherit the kingdom of God" (1 Cor. 6:9, 10, NASB). "But for the cowardly and unbelieving and abominable and murderers and immoral persons and sorcerers and idolaters and all liars, their part will be in the lake that burns with fire and brimstone, which is the second death" (Rev. 21:8, NASB). The encouraging and wonderful truth in this listing of the lost is that they still have hope of Heaven because God has said, "And such were some of you: but ye are washed, but ye are sanctified, but ye are justified in the name of the Lord Jesus, and by the Spirit of our God" (1 Cor. 6:11).

Rejection—Lest it appear that only religious people will enter God's Heaven and that the restrictions are lifted if one simply tries to be religious and do good, listen to the words of Jesus spoken in the Sermon on the Mount, "Not every one that saith unto me, Lord, Lord, shall enter into the kingdom of heaven; but he that doeth the will of my Father which is in heaven. Many will say to me in that day, Lord, Lord, have we not prophesied in thy name? and in thy name have cast out devils? and in thy name done many wonderful works? And then will I profess unto them, I never knew you: depart from me, ye that work iniquity" (Matt. 7:21–23). Good works by those who have not received Jesus Christ as their Savior not only will not permit them to enter Heaven, but they will also generally make Heaven farther away. One who depends on his religious works sees no need of trusting Christ for eternal life. Heaven is restricted. There is no admittance unless one comes by God's way. "The way of the cross leads home."

It is imperative for each of us to recognize that someday we shall leave this world. We shall spend eternity someplace. Not all who die will go to Heaven. It is restricted and reserved for God's people.

Is My Name Written There?

Lord, I care not for riches,
Neither silver nor gold—
I would make sure of heaven,
I would enter the fold.
In the book of Thy kingdom
With its pages so fair,
Tell me, Jesus my Savior,
Is my name written there?

Lord, my sins they are many,
Like the sands of the sea,
But Thy blood, O my Savior,
Is sufficient for me;
For Thy promise is written
In bright letters that glow,
"Though your sins be as scarlet,
I will make them like snow."

O, that beautiful city,
With its mansions of light,
With its glorified beings
In pure garments of white;
Where no evil thing cometh
To despoil what is fair,
Where the angels are watching—
Yes, my name's written there.

—Mary A. Kidder (1820–1905)

CHAPTER 19

Heaven, a Place of Reservation

"Get Your Ticket Early"

If you expect to go to Heaven, you must have a reservation—and before the hour you intend to arrive. Have you ever tried to find a hotel room on earth where a crowd was gathering? When you asked for a room without a reservation, the answer was, "Sorry, every room is taken." Then the traveler in a similar situation looks for a room in another motel. He may or may not find one. Heaven, however, has no extra rooms. Nor does it have any other motels down the way. There is only one way to get to Heaven; you must have a previous reservation if you expect to spend eternity there. "But ye are come unto mount Sion, and unto the city of the living God, the heavenly Jerusalem, and to an innumerable company of angels, to the general assembly and church of the firstborn, which are written in heaven, and to God the Judge of all, and to the spirits of just men made perfect" (Heb. 12:22, 23).

Little five-year-old Allen Sparks moved from Clarksville, Texas, to Little Rock, Arkansas. He and a newly found friend began to discuss grandparents. Allen boasted that he had a grandfather in Heaven. His new friend responded with the revelation that he had two grandfathers in Heaven and then questioned, "Do you suppose our grandfathers know each other up there?"

"Of course not!" young Allen disgustedly replied. "My grandfather is in a Texas heaven!"

CHAPTER 19

The Bible makes it undeniably clear that there is only *one* Heaven and only *one* way to get there. A sinner must have a reservation by trusting the One Who said, "I am *the* way, *the* truth, and *the* life: *no man cometh unto the Father, but by me*" (John 14:6). You see, entrance into Heaven will not depend upon your color, creed, affiliation or country, but upon your personal relationship with Christ as your Savior. "Verily, verily, I say unto thee, Except a man be born again, he cannot see the kingdom of God. Marvel not that I said unto thee, Ye must be born again" (John 3:3, 7). "And there shall in no wise enter into it anything that defileth, neither whatsoever worketh abomination, or maketh a lie: but they which are written in the Lamb's book of life" (Rev. 21:27).

After the American space program landed a man on the moon, a church posted the following announcement on the bulletin board outside the church building: "We have reached the moon. Now let us reach Heaven. Get your flight training here." Thank God for every church engaged in the great privilege of providing "flight training for Heaven." In so doing, these people make the way plain so that lost sinners can have reservations to spend eternity there.

Paul, the great example of New Testament preachers, declared that Christ is the only way to Heaven. "Moreover, brethren, I declare unto you the gospel which I preached unto you, which also ye have received, and wherein ye stand; by which also ye are saved, if ye keep in memory what I preached unto you, unless ye have believed in vain. For I delivered unto you first of all that which I also received, how that Christ died for our sins according to the scriptures" (1 Cor. 15:1–3). "Be it known unto you therefore, men and brethren, that through this man is preached unto you the forgiveness of sins: And by him all that believe are justified from all things, from which ye could not be justified by the law of Moses" (Acts 13:38, 39). "But even though we, or an angel from heaven, should preach to you a gospel contrary to that which we have preached to you, let him be accursed" (Gal. 1:8, NASB).

Why did Paul insist that the gospel—the death, burial and resurrection of Christ—be preached to all men? Paul knew, and down deep in our hearts we all know, that Jesus Christ is the only way one can be saved and can know he has a reservation in Heaven.

When the Roll Is Called up Yonder

When the trumpet of the Lord shall sound and time shall be
    no more,
And the morning breaks eternal, bright and fair—
When the saved of earth shall gather over on the other shore,
And the roll is called up yonder I'll be there!

On that bright and cloudless morning when the dead in
    Christ shall rise
And the glory of His resurrection share—
When His chosen ones shall gather to their home beyond
    the skies,
And the roll is called up yonder—I'll be there!

Let us labor for the Master from the dawn till setting sun,
Let us talk of all His wondrous love and care;
Then when all of life is over and our work on earth is done,
And the roll is called up yonder I'll be there!

—James M. Black, 1893 (1856–1938)

Heaven, a Place of Residence

"Home Sweet Home"

A residence is a place of abode; a dwelling; a permanent habitation. Though God's people live on this earth, their eternal home is Heaven, a more permanent home than anything they have in this world. While we wait to go Home, we are assured of being a resident of Heaven now. "For our citizenship is in heaven, from which also we eagerly wait for a Savior, the Lord Jesus Christ" (Phil. 3:20, NASB). The Greek word for citizenship came *to* refer to a colony of foreigners who, though living outside their own country, lived according to the laws of the country from whence they had come.

Every child of God is now a citizen of Heaven and therefore must live according to Heaven's regulations. To be the land of "heavenly citizens" we ought to be demands knowledge of the Word of God, much prayer and personal commitment to Christ. Otherwise we may become so heavenly minded that we are no earthly good. A good citizen of Heaven never forgets he has a permanent residence there; he will be the best and most influential visitor or ambassador for Christ on earth.

Christians must act like citizens of Heaven act. But how can they do that? God has made a wonderful provision for His people, though temporarily away from their residence in Heaven, to live on earth as though they were there. He sent the Holy Spirit to enable us to live Heaven on earth. Jesus said, "And I will pray the Father, and he shall give you another Comforter, that he may abide with you for ever; even the Spirit of truth. . . . He dwelleth with you, and shall be in you" (John 14:16, 17). The Comforter is the One Who has been "called alongside" to help the earthly resident of Heaven so that his life will be filled with heaven's purity, peace and patience.

Purity—The inhabitants of Heaven will wear white robes (Rev. 7:9). These are saints out of the Great Tribulation "and have washed their robes, and made them white in the blood of the Lamb" (Rev. 7:13, 14). Thank God "the blood washes white, but never whitewashes." White symbolizes purity or holiness. Therefore, if we have our residence in Heaven, we should live lives of holiness on earth. God says, "Be holy . . . in all your behavior . . . You shall be holy; for I am holy . . ." (1 Pet. 1:15, 16, NASB; cf. Rev. 14:4, 5; Rev. 3:5, 6).

Peace—The victorious saints in the Great Tribulation are seen by John not only clothed in white robes but also with "palms in their hands" (Rev. 7:9), a symbol of peace through victory. A. C. Dixon wrote, "Through Jesus Christ, they have been reconciled to God and gained victory over sin. There is no discordant note in their nature. They love God's will and way, they do his pleasure—peace reigns like a king because everyone does the will of the King." Heaven has no hatred, envy, jealousy or selfish ambition. Now as representatives on earth, we should "have peace one with another" (Mark 9:50; Col. 3:15). The Christian is to "follow after the things which make for peace" (Rom. 14:19). The "fruit of the Spirit is . . . peace" (Gal. 5:22). The future residents of Heaven now have and manifest peace because Christ has already won the battle!

Patience—Those in Heaven who will come out of the Great Tribulation will be "a great multitude, which no man could number," and they will stand before the throne, and will see God upon the throne (Rev. 7:9–15). Christ is pictured in Heaven ". . . at the right hand of God, waiting . . . until His enemies be made a footstool for His feet" (Heb. 10:12, 13, NASB). The eternal God on His throne and the living Christ waiting for the final assured victory tell us Heaven is characterized by patience. Since our citizenship is there, we should be patient on earth knowing the God Who controls all things cannot make a mistake. "Let us run with patience the race that is set before us" (Heb. 12:1). Christians, let us never forget that we are citizens of Heaven. We have a residence there. Let us live and act like citizens of Heaven while we are waiting to go Home.

Dear reader, eternity is inevitable. Heaven and Hell are realities. Where we spend eternity depends on the decision we make regarding the Lord Jesus Christ. Have you rejected Him, or have you received Him as Savior? He said, "I am the way, the truth and the life: No man cometh unto the Father, but by me" (John 14:6). "Neither is there salvation in any other: for there is none other name under heaven given among men, whereby we must be saved" (Acts 4:12). If you have not already trusted Him as your Savior, will you do so now? Humbly tell Him you are a lost sinner and ask Him to save you. God's promises assure you that He will take away the penalty of your sin and set you free. Then you will be ready to travel with His redeemed people to that eternal abiding place called Heaven. Together we can sing the following song:

O, That Will Be Glory

When all my labors and trials are o'er
And I am safe on that beautiful shore,
Just to be near the dear Lord I adore
Will through the ages be glory for me.

When, by the gift of His infinite grace,
I am accorded in heaven a place,
Just to be there and to look on His face
Will through the ages be glory for me.

Joy like a river around me will flow;
Friends will be there I have loved long ago;
Yet, just a smile from my Saviour, I know,
Will through the ages be glory for me.

—Charles H. Gabriel, 1900 (1856–1952) (Copyright 1972
    by Alfred B. Smith in *Living Hymns*)